Michèle Roberts was born in England, and is half-French and half-English. She has been poetry editor of *Spare Rib* and *City Limits*, and is author of two volumes of poetry, *The Mirror of the Mother* (1986) and *Psyche and the Hurricane* (1990). She is also known as a novelist; her novel *Daughters of the House* (Virago 1992) was shortlisted for the Booker Prize and won the WH Smith Literary Award. She has written six other novels: *A Piece of the Night* (1978), *The Visitation* (1983), *The Wild Girl* (1984), *The Book of Mrs Noah* (1987), *In the Red Kitchen* (1990) and *Flesh and Blood*, (Virago 1994), her most recent novel. Virago also publishes her collection of stories *During Mother's Absence* (1993).

Michèle Roberts lives in London and in France.

D0715606

All the selves I was

new and selected poems

Michèle Roberts

Published by VIRAGO PRESS Limited, March 1995
20 Vauxhall Bridge Road, London SW1 2SA

A CIP catalogue record for this book
is available from the British Library

Printed and bound in Great Britain by
Cox & Wyman Ltd, Reading, Berkshire

Acknowledgements

Some of these poems have previously appeared in the following magazines, collections and anthologies:

Angels of Fire, Apples and Snakes, Aquarius, Arvon International Poetry Competition 1987 anthology, Bête Noir, Blue Nose anthology, Bread and Roses, British Council New Writing 3, Certain Gestures, City Limits, Cutlasses and Earrings, Critical Quarterly, First and Always, Jacaranda Review, Licking the Bed Clean, New Statesman, One Foot on the Mountain, Only Poetry, Smile Smile Smile Smile, So This Is Love, Tampa Review, The Third Eye, The Left and the Erotic, The Politics of Spirit, Touch Papers.

Author's note

I should like to thank all the many friends who have supported and encouraged my poetry over the years; Anne McDermid of Curtis Brown; everyone at Virago, especially Melanie Silgardo; and Jim Latter.

for Jim, always

Contents

from *The mirror of the mother* (1986)

from
The mirror of the mother (1986)

bangkok breakfast

the monk
stands
under a flowering tree

prodigal with sweetness

women come women go
and come with earthen pots
to fill his, thus their own
torn flesh of priestlessness

lacking substance they
subsist on his
spare shadow
stain his robes
which burn with sacrifice
to make their merit
                          food
and beggar both they give
men and children suck
for their salvation
                          their
coin of vile body
seeds the ground
                    prodigal
with sweetness

under a flowering tree
the monk
stands

judith and delilah and me

when holofernes slept
then it was
that judith slew him
with his own sword
by her hand

when samson slept
then it was
that his strength left him
his own hair
by delilah's hand

before you sleep
I shall come before you, wet
and naked utterly, our
own bodies shall be
our pavilion, you shall not
need to wound me
to escape

then
o fearful lion of judah
see
I shall take your sword
into my mouth, I
shall lay my head
inside your mouth
samson carrying gates is lonely
lay your hands upon
my gates, grasp
my hair, bury
your sword, your fingernails
clotted with sweet wax
taste
the honeycomb
between my lion's jaws

judith returned home
married and bore six sons
became perhaps
an intolerable shrew
delilah at sixty
still has to
dance for a living

the big man

I want to spin you, big man
make you skip
hop, twirl on nimble toes
I want to whip you like a top
my tongue lashing you
with ropes of silk
till you unfurl
flags, flowers, parasols

I want to be a crazy blackbird
singing all night lewd
riddles to your smiling ear

won't you make my blood
jump? won't you
step along up there
clowning and glittering
beneath the big top, and
see me stretched out here
your fine strong net
with nothing on but jewels?

boom! go the drums of sweat
as neon bodies wink

big man, you hold me in your hands
big man, you warm me with your tender flesh
I am a bee hauling honey out
a fly tickling a slow fish

tulips

the clamped bud
splits, green armour clangs
down, raw scarlet silk
flares like a parachute

the petals' mouth
those red doors
the way in

stamens and pistils burst
up, each sticky velvet brush
gold pollen glistens on
their black fur tips

deep winy heart
as dark as raspberries
for plundering wasps

translucent sun-traps
colour running like a hot
streak of shiny sweet
juice in tossing cups

season of passionate red
opening, red
festival of flames and tongues

the woman who wanted to be a hero

the first task was to persuade them
a woman could go
that my heart could and did ring
like warrior drums
that I could curtsey to dragons
and then slay them
that I could leap seven leagues
at the drop of a high-heeled boot
my mother and father complained
there was no farewell ritual for me
but I had brand-new disguises
and I needed to go

the second task was to search
in a dark wood for years
alone, and afraid, and not knowing
whether I touched
men, or gnarled trees, or hobgoblins
still, I learned songs, and the way of the wild
and the wise witch showed me
the way out of the wood

the third and hardest task
is letting you search for me
through thorns, over glass-topped walls
past siren music
and the sleepy drugs of flowers
I must stand still, I must wait
wet, humming aloud, smelling
sweet, smelling strong

certainly, I have few words
and no tricks
for this

Magnificat
(for Sian, after thirteen years)

oh this man
what a meal he made of me
how he chewed and gobbled and sucked

in the end he spat me all out

you arrived on the dot, in the nick
of time, with your red curls flying
I was about to slip down the sink like grease
I nearly collapsed, I almost
wiped myself out like a stain
I called for you, and you came, you voyaged
fierce as a small archangel with swords and breasts
you declared the birth of a new life
in my kitchen there was an annunciation
and I was still, awed by your hair's glory

you commanded me to sing of my redemption

oh my friend, how
you were mother for me, and how
I could let myself lean on you
comfortable as an old cloth, familiar as enamel saucepans
I was a child again, pyjamaed
in winceyette, my hair plaited, and you
listened, you soothed me like cakes and milk
you listened to me for three days, and I poured
it out, I flowed all over you
like wine, like oil, you touched the place where it hurt
at night we slept together in my big bed
your shoulder eased me towards dreams

when we met, I tell you
it was a birthday party, a funeral
it was a holy communion
between women, a Visitation

it was two old she-goats butting
and nuzzling each other in the smelly fold

madwoman at Rodmell

(for Sylvia Plath)

she strolls in the valley, alone
her ears scan the warning
twanging of birds
her boots plop and suck in the mud's grip

the sky is a cold gold spoon
sun tart and sweet
in the cup of hills licked
clean by the gulp of cows
– at the cup's lip, the foam
and crust of milk, a swell of clouds
and yellow plums; leaves curl
like the peel in marmalade

the world is her mouth
a sour swill of yells

trees scar, and suddenly
redden; bright berries of blood and teeth
hang in the hedge; the bad
baby is out; she
bites through the net; she swarms
free, fizzing; she thunders like bees in a box
maddened for honey, and her mama

her lips clang shut on mean rations:
she swallows the river
and mourns on down, a thin bellyful

Irish prisoners of war

this is the last battleground
their skin is a thin barricade

once, they were rosy mouths at mother's breast
once, they were white milk in a flask of flesh
now that sweetness dries, now their mouths are
stoppered up: the tender leather
of wineskins shrinks
to bags of gristle and sticks

war has boarded their bodies up
and they have flares, not eyes
that burn indifferently
through newsprint, onto our TV screens
no patrol can put that fire out
that consumes their citadel

under their barbed-wire crowns
their souls snarl out:
yellow smears along the walls
they are the holy ones, the lonely anchorites
well schooled in crucifixion, by their priests

wild men, naked, on the blanket
wild women, starving for what
new mothering?

after my grandmother's death

each day is a full
spool, and death winds me in
her foot tap, taps
rocking the cradle

death is mrs moon, death is a spry spinster
I am a thread the moon spins with
and I come reeling in from my grief-stricken dance

the moon puts silver on grandmother's eyes
in her nostrils she puts the cold perfume of death
– moonspider spinning shrouds and swaddling bands

my mother's womb spun me a fine cocoon
spun me round and out, death tugged
my umbilical cord, she grinned
and tied me into her weaving

the moon who eats babies on winter nights
has her dark face, and rubbery hands
but grandmother rescued me
and held me close, she shone
steady for me, then I felt so blessed

then death strode out
trawling, trawling
and grandmother was mackerel to her silver net

the womb is the house of death
and each woman
spins in death's web; as I inch
back to the light
death pays out the bright thread

lament for my grandmother on the day of the winter solstice

woman who cradled me, and made me rise
I am bread, you were yeast and salt in me

sometimes, my grandmother, you were busy dying
and your body became a box of bones
that travels towards the furnace to be crushed and burnt

we have surrounded a rose tree with your ashes
between turf lips you lie compressed
a word in a green tongue

when your hip smashed, fragile bone enduring whole
for almost a hundred years
you consented to darkness

you were dismayed, but you consented to death
with some struggle, and you told me:
there is no heaven, there is just us together here now

you closed your eyes and slipped off
(and I wasn't with you)
you tunnelled down through the bedclothes
prisoner of pain you dug an alley down
and then you cut loose and left me alone

most nights, you told me,
you dreamed of your dead husband
love long lost, and you complained to him:
where are you, lover? where have you gone?

my fists thunder on your breast
the bony gate to Hades and the ribbed boat
that takes your spirit there
I harrow Hell, calling out for you lost in the dark

the resurrection, the incorruptible flesh
how you doubted that, watching yourself slowly die
noting the new frailties, your body rotting
to enrich the earth

where are you now, my grandmother, white-
haired warrior, indefatigable voyager?
your pine coffin was the boat you chose to launch
and death the great water it furthered you to cross

you sailed off with just one bunch
of red and yellow flowers
you huddled in a wooden coracle
and disembarked in flames

you tow me after you
you make me grow on up
and now I am one step nearer to death
and that deep sea
where you rock through the year's long night

poem on the day of the spring equinox

the winter enters her
so silent, it
slants in and
squats her; the
thin time of Lent
her skin's a curtain between cold and cold

naked, she fills up with the city snow
and frozen trash; she's a container
for rain-pocked slush and the brown
mash at the gutter's edge; the cold
moulds her, bleak in the park

there's no prince, no melting
kiss; she simply
endures
the dark months
of the occupation, the aching embrace
– like a root

till March loosens her

then there's a white
insurrection
of crocuses; each one blooms
close and full as an egg; how
their purity hurts

she must learn to open her yellow heart

winter sacrament

last night I met my mother again
at the altar steps, in the cathedral vault
we knelt on stone, our chins upturned
we were open-mouthed, awaiting
the body's guest:
the trusty bread, unleavened
delicate as frost

it's a dream, I thought
when I woke up: the street
was absent, a
blank page of whiteness, shops
and cars sunk
under a soft blotter of snow
– tiny, circular wafers of ice
tinkled and whirled at my lips

later, the brilliant moon
in the dark night; cold
and solid as plate
she shone, and her silver hands
dressed the bare trees
– the pavement outside the locked church
was a rink to slip home across

in bed, I shiver and fast
in a snowfield of sheets
lonely for you, my absent guest
our snowflake bodies
melting on each other's tongues
– the true communion

poem on St Valentine's Day

the diagnosis complete, I tried to become
a surgeon, deciding to operate:
I imagined white tiles, a single
whack of the axe, our bodies'
severance, our selves falling
cleanly apart

but rather than simply
rip myself off
from your skin, patiently
I've had to unpick every stitch
that binds us, snipping
at catgut that cries like violins
to the scissors' percussion

thus I expose the wound
red and raw to the february wind

I keep wanting to tell you
how much separation hurts, to re-
entwine, ask you
to be bandage and comforter

this women's work is thrifty and grim:
learning to save myself, learning to live
alone through the long winter nights
means so much unknotting, unknitting
unravelling, untying the mother-cord
– so much undoing

rite de passage

(for Joan of Arc)

it is always the quiet ones
whom the whirlwind picks:
Joan, thrust from dumb worship
of forests, God's fist at her back
the saints articulating
her bones to an iron
syntax, the ringing logic of mail

once she danced in wordless circles
of girls, hands linked, once she hung
leaf-loops, flowers in knots
on trees, her invocation
a green twist, a perfect O

then the vision plucked her away
and sentenced her: the voices
insisted she marry, and name
the new part of herself: war's
rhetorician, she stammered
embracing the angel, faint in his angular grip

Joan, after that meeting
returned to broken places: compatriots hurt
by her eyes'
pure androgynous glare; turning
her face from family, she forswore
silence and mother-tongues

yet, in the end, after victories
after the failed leap from the tower
she was trapped: ecclesiastical
grammar, the rope of deft priests, tied
and tripped her; she conjugated
their only available verb: I confess
to heresy; I am unnatural

they pitied her: duped
peasant, illiterate girl
and duly they sent her back
to the smoking green wood, the sharp tree
– lashed to it, burning, a human garland
poor freak (born too soon) she carried on
crying out messages they could not hear

Persephone descends to the underworld

1.
how could I ever make a friend
of death? though he behaves
like one: dropping in unannounced

he wears a lover's face, which
touches mine; his garden
smells of rain and summer, here
at night, we sit; he
cuts an avocado pear in half; we
eat green flesh and suck the stone
between us; then we dance; when
he arrives in bed I call it rape

last winter I fled from him
back north to the speechless
waterfall, back to immaculate ice; I
preferred white perfection, I
preferred to remain intact; I sang this
loudly enough for him to hear

this spring my lover
came for me again; this
time my mother did not
hold me back; she blessed me; she
suggested it
was about time; then she released my wrist

my lover is a dark man
we embrace in the garden, in the grave; his
twisting root is clotted with my black earth
as I break open, and take him in

this time no return is possible; this
time he has me; this time when we go
underground we go together
though I shall be crying loudly
for the mother and women lovers I leave behind

2.
in the beginning, I was
carried away by him; helpless; he
welcomed me, and I fell forwards, down
into the depths of him; he
opened up for me; he
made me die, and die

down here it is dark, so dark
apart from the glitter of amethysts
which he breaks off for me
like a flowering branch; he piles my lap
with ammonites, offers me
iron pyrites
phalluses, intricate coral fans

there are days when I shiver at all this
glistening rock he
strokes more kindly than my skin, turn
from his fools' gold, strain
for a lost body, lost light, lost voice

days when my forest
petrifies, and I'm the fossil
woman who resists
his hammer, his chisel, his collector's hands

also there are nights
when his black coal head
lies next to mine, nights when my heart
drums as the twin of his, my breath and blood
in tune with his, learning to sing
of friendship; a difficult, a new
benediction

Demeter grieving

Demeter has torn off
her yellow linen dress. Its fallen
ruffles drift along the grass.

The beech wood crouches on the slope
dark and shiny; its henna'ed mass
Demeter's hair, which hoods her wet face.

Demeter beats her fists together. Chestnuts
and oaks explode in rhythms of red
pink, russet. Bruises burst on her skin.

Demeter howls: wind cutting the reeds.
Only a mallard shrieks back
here, where the light is watery and thin.

Demeter wraps herself in a black storm
cloak. The afternoon pales, draining
away down winter's throat.

Demeter weeps:
her child's lost
Persephone's gone.

Persephone voyages

I travel through burning
streets of yellow façades and small
blackened palaces. I measure
the city that swims, the lion city
of carved pink islands and smelly
canals. Every alley leads to his bed.

So many women have gone
down before me into the dark.
Will I plunge up again? Shall
I be born from these water corridors?

Twilight. I am lost in the wild
garden, alone, the swish of chilly
grass on my ankles, night beginning
to coat the acanthus leaves. I turn
and run in a privet labyrinth. At its
heart, a shock: a green room
where the dead
dance in white marble, a nymph shrieking.

No way out. Behind me
in the doorway of cypresses
the man in black.

No use remembering
my mother's walled slope
of flowering orchards, lettuce
and artichoke beds, the bells
that juggle and toss
in a copper bowl held
between the hills' blue knees
the rhythm of her breathing as she sleeps.

Demeter keeps going

(for my mother)

This wood is Demeter's golden house
the sun slaps wet paint on, and
here the goddess tramps about, busy beneath
her skylight of chestnut leaves
yellow and luminous as glass.

She whistles loudly enough
to shake the trees, smiles at the soft
crash and rattle of nuts
into her lap, inserts her fingernail
to split and prise off the spiky husks.

She sorts and inspects her glossy
harvest, the kernels' truth. She
tests each seed with her teeth: sweet
or bitter, the taste of rain or rot
the smell of sap or the sour kiss of decay.

She regrets the spoilt fruit, but
labours doggedly on, stocking the hollow
bellies of oaks. Then, larders full
she packs down leaf mould, rotten
nuts in a compost dance: death is no waste.

She chooses the best of the season's goods
to plant, then squats on the moist
black earth and puts her ear
to the chestnut's bark. She listens for messages
issuing up from the roots, the invisible girl.

Demeter sleeps in her house of twigs
curled under frosty quilts. She dreams
that the coldness will pass, that the barren
fields will stiffen with corn.
She prays that her buried daughter may rise.

She waits for Persephone to return.

Persephone pays a visit to Demeter

Suddenly I allow myself
more than a single room: this year
I explore the whole house, pace
its roof and stairs. All its windows
stand open. All its planks are bare. Salt
lines their crevices. I hear them
gossip at night.

We have restored this house. All
the major repairs are done. Now
we are tidying up, inspecting corners
from attic to cellar. The spiders help us
spinning their webs and sucking up flies.

We lean on a windowsill, looking out
over the estuary and the sea. The sun
flattens the fishermen who crawl across
the skin of the deep. Turning, you display
your newly short white crop. And I
show you my first grey hair.

I'm like one of those boats down there
siren bawling with grief: I'm going back
mother, this time I really mean it
I'm really going.

Persephone gives birth

in the enormous field
tight with corn, the stiff
jostle of stalks, gold arrows
pouring over the hill, heads pressing
Demeter's waist, their heavy tips
cutting her hands that she holds
up and out, hostage
to the harvest and the heat

she beats a path through
she parts the gold waves
she hurries
the cornfield resists

in the churchyard
Persephone in her bone nightgown
squats down

the oyster woman
(in memoriam Helen Smith)

the corpse filed away in a tin drawer
of the state brain resurrects
herself: a hiccup, a sour taste
on the legal tongue

the pathologist, the surgeon, the policeman, the coroner
chew over the meaning of *victim*, of *innocence*
there is indignation, there is gnashing of teeth
analysis shows
there is genital injury, head abrasions
and bruises, which are consistent with rape

their lips kiss the book, will speak truth
her lips are sealed; who kissed
her lips, who tore them?

certainly she was born
and slapped, and breathed
possibly she was drunk
and slapped, and sobered
possibly she was hysterical
and slapped, and shut up
possibly she indulged in sexual horseplay
and slapped his face, certainly she died

analysis shows
the woman on the couch is hysterical
she cries: I am dismembered
I am pulled apart by guilt and knowledge
I cannot remember anything about it
I cannot bear to, I cannot bear witness
I have taken leave of all my senses, I was not there
I shall cover my face

the daughter under the sheet
on the mortuary slab
is vowed to chastity and silence
the mother on the marble mattress in church
has lost her daughter, and has died in childbed
their shrouds, their wedding veils dissolve
into the salt swaddling bands of the sea

deep buried, the oyster sits
on the gravel bed men have dug for her
their fingers fret at her frilled
stone petticoats: they wish to culture her
her valves open in welcome; they insert grit
her valves close; our mouths bleed, and are full of rocks

the woman on the couch goes home
and reads the morning papers
in bed, the cave of her becoming
rolling her tongue over jagged words
she remembers the sea, her mother
she re-members herself, she is forced to become a poet
she is forced to bear witness, to defend herself
then from the injuries inflicted she creates pearls

investigation shows
the details of the injuries inflicted
were omitted at the first hearing
the decision to omit them had been taken
in order not to distress her father
because they were not relevant

knowledge of the body is not relevant?
but the body resurrects itself, and returns
home in a tin boat, borne across the sea
which stutters over and over
at jagged logical rocks
which interrupts the chatter of death
sentences with staccato pearls

at the first hearing of our words
our willingness to admit inside knowledge
to admit that we were there, that we were witnesses
that we could speak of it, caused much distress

in order that
the pathologist, the surgeon, the policeman, the coroner
may have clean hands, may return home
to lie
between clean sheets, to dream of clean
daughters and filthy whores

This poem refers to the death of a young nurse, Helen Smith, in mysterious
and never fully explained circumstances, in Saudi Arabia in 1983, and to the
controversy at the inquest on the cause of her death. Some of the lines of
the poem are lifted directly from newspaper reports of the case at the time.

on Highbury Hill

that girl
with her sharp
hips, pelvic bones
pointed like sycamore
leaves, she
with her boy's crop, hair
cut short as stubble in the corn
fields where fire and smoke
begin, scarlet heaps of burning
that collapse softly to black ash

she unexpectedly
came running out
of darkness, past
the iron spears of railings
the rattle of shadows guarding the park

suddenly I remembered her: she
whom I lost, hidden
for years in mists like this one, a
shiver of silver along the street
september night arriving
cold and solid as a gun

after a decade of absence

frost on the pavement
edge, evening air a chilly
second skin, my mouth
open, the wind in my throat
desire quickening me

her gift to me

Before this, I was sucking
at death's breast, gasping for more
whey as bitter as soot. I
gagged on spoonfuls of ash.

I paused, I gathered my skirts, raced upwards
dropping the world. I hung on and flew. To the dream city
I always believed in: true, though invisible
like the kingdom of God.

Down again. Crushed. I crawled the sidewalk grids
the repeated intersection strobe. Giants played Monopoly:
skyscrapers for dice, the green dollar bills of Central Park.
The food was fake, chic plastic suppers for dolls.

Everybody wanted so much, including me.
The rich ate the poor, then shat them into the subways
and the junkies' eyes were derelict lots, reflecting
the needles of syringe buildings poking at a lost skin.

Rescue. Down West Eleventh Street
a woman sat on her front
steps combing a cat. When she looked
at me I saw her black tadpole eyes.

She waved her fist, and the houses suddenly stopped.
She opened her palm and breathed
and the sky sprang up and out
uncreased, enormous, wholly blue. Her miracle.

The wind uncorked my mouth
and the Hudson river poured in.
I abandoned myself like a coat
and the river flowed through me.

We walked on the water, the salty wooden tongue
of the rotting pier, in a swarm of light.
She hugged herself like a secret sea:
'Once, here, we saw an albatross.'

In the cab cantering up Fifth Avenue, waltzing
from lane to lane with yellow grace
God sat beside me on the leatherette seat
and the driver sang to the wheel: 'go, baby, go.'

Along the New Jersey turnpike I rocked, straphanging
with both hands in the glass bus.
Oil refineries and trees streamed through my eyes and skin.
The hill of God inside and out. The end of me.

babysitting

(for Sarah)

October burns my stuttering tongue.
The sky is a warm whisky glass
that pours light, and the chestnut trees
are alive twice: glittering
domes that lift off, soft
explosions, rust and pink confetti
litter blurs the grass.

I wheel your son out, over
the grey breath of pavement
stencilled with the memory of plane leaves
soon to be frosted hard and white
as china plates. He fists
an arc of yellow plasticine:
'moon' he says: 'banana. Letter C.'

Later, from the train, I mark
the broken brown diamonds of fields
the black and white jigsaw of cows.
Illiterate, I can't decipher the waxy red
scrawl on the right-hand window, till the sun
suddenly prints it out, shadow-writing
on the opposite pane: 'beware: lovers at large.'

I remember how we played with the baby
rolling him, naked, to and fro between us
on your marital bed, like a cylindrical
seal I'd stamped with a new myth of
longing, belonging.

Penelope awaits the return of Ulysses

1.
This morning, at nine,
opening the front door of our flat
onto the first-floor landing, I found
snow fallen in the house.

Silently, overnight, the stairs'
concertina angles were flattened
and smoothed out. No carpet but a
white drift between white walls.

The decorator trod in with
his glistening brushes, his tin
slopping cream paint. He swaddled the
banisters in cotton bandages, hushed me.

All afternoon I have been laying
new lino in the kitchen, its pattern
of white squares glossy as béchamel
flowing between my hands.

Snow is falling in me. My house
has splintered. This grief
can't be blotted by white dustsheets
or covered up by pearl vinyl.

2.
Above me that enormous silver mouth
mumbling on pins. A sort of aunt
counting her cross-stitch sewn
along the raw edges of sleep.

Night-boat pushes through darkness.
Cargo of tangled threads I try
in the morning to gloss into words.
This is the dream-work: to weave, to unweave.

My sisters learned to layer white
cotton for quilts, how to smock petticoats.
I pricked my finger, imagined, in coloured wools
a hessian garden where lovers kissed.

Why should I mend the torn linen sheets
of our bed, rip them in half, turn them
sides to middle, hem them again?
I make the best of everything I can.

Your absence undoes me.
I want to make, and make.
These days, I want to remain unfinished.
I need you to hear me out. To unravel me.

New Year's Eve at Lavarone

The world is reversed. Gone into negative.
Pale monochrome of peaks, a white lid
on the lake, the valley newly scooped out
of white blocks then speckled with brown
grains. Pines bristle thinly
on the mountain's flank. Each black branch
is lined exactly with white like cut plush.
White fur paws of spruce trees.

We push up into steep woods. Our toecaps
cut steps in the blank ramp ahead. Walls
of snow plot the curve of the vanished
track. What were meadows are now full
wedges of white we plough across, knee-deep.
Behind us, our scribbles on winter's diagram.
Under our boots, the creak of snow's broken
crust; below that, the rustle of layers of manuscript.

The forest's a palimpsest, a folk-tale.
Some of its actors' names we recover from
fragile prints: hare, squirrel, fox, goat.
Others we guess at: this white blot might be
a badger's sett. Here is a magic tree
ribbed solid with icicles, dripping
candles of water. Here are white logs
laid out like dead brides.

Our narrator, the man in the red woollen cap
leads us to the myth's heart. He scrapes with his
stick in a white dip, exposes a perfect circle
of glazed grey ice. He uncovers the mirror
of the mother, she who goes away
comes back, goes away. Her cold eye blinks
unblinks. Our kiss on her round mouth is chalk,
inscribes us on her body's blackboard: want, want.

Next March, he tells us, all
the whiteness of these hills
will loosen, will slide off
like a nightdress, like a shroud.

Train journey Shrewsbury-Aberystwyth

Violet earth, green fuzz of grass.
Bright sticks fill the ditches, oildrums pile
next to a swamp rosy with pigs.

Under the elms, the graves are tidy bright
packets of seed laid out in a patience game.
The dead wear florals and do not care.

Snail churches crawl up the hills.
Sheep with red numbers stamped on their backs
lambs in black stockings, spill down the slope

fallen white petals. Chickens
scuttle and flap. Now the hills
swoop and leap, swell to mountains.

At every village stop, women and babies
are suddenly visible. The guardsvan disgorges
them, hung about with pushchairs and shopping.

The mothers have stood all the way
in the rattling dark. We rush away from them
as though we have taken vows

of freedom, instability, unchastity.
Single, as serious as brides
we hurtle towards the same deep bed.

On Boulogne Sands

(a painting by Philip Wilson Steer)

Le ciel est bleu.

Monique, the eldest, skinny and awkward in corsets, dark plait dropping straight as a plumb-line down her blue jacket, stares at the red and white striped bathing-machines. Stout men in navy wool splash in, the cold sea slopping over their shoulders. What is it like? She imagines a transformation total as baptism, her own voice crying out as she drowns. Today, being unwell, she is forbidden to swim.

La mer est vaste. Le soleil brille,

Frederique tucks up her scarlet skirt and white flounced petticoat, unpeels black stockings from legs creamy as stripped willow-sticks. She hops across the scooped-out hollows of the rocks, slipping on sopping green feathery moss, dips her feet into pools walled with limpets. Her heart is a pale crab jerking from side to side. She cocks an ear for the voices calling her back.

parmi les nuages blancs.

Marthe collects pebbles pale as eggs, smooth grey banded with charcoal and veined with mauve, speckled with glittery quartz. She picks up stiff dead starfish, seaweed in puckered rubber strips, parched and bleached cuttle-bones, mackerel-blue mussel shells opening like wings. Smuggled home in her pocket, the beach will lie under her in bed all night long. Glass waves rising and falling. Slither of water over dragged stones.

Il fait beau.

Chantal, the youngest, in a goffered white cotton sun-bonnet and pink smock, squats to prod the mound of sand she has dug, distended as Maman's belly. She carves out a moat in the wet sludge, then a shallow channel that runs to the edge of the sea. Connects them. Watches the cloudy waters rush in, surge and wash around the castle. Smash! she flattens it.

En vacances.

Lily Mount, the English governess, struggles to fill in the daily blank in her journal with halting French words. Her straw hat is looped with daisies and delphiniums, her pale hair puffed out at the sides. She would like to throw herself into the sea like a message in a bottle: save me. Soon it will be tea-time: lemonade in tin cups, fresh bread and bitter chocolate. The wind blows sand into her eyes, salt onto her lips.

Je voudrais. Je veux. Je manque de pratique.

America assaults my mouth

We stumble up a ramp of air.
The rouged hostess dissolves
yellow grit and ice
in paper cups, doles out sweaty
fettucine, beef shavings in glue sauce.
The sky is blue as an apron.

The kitchen's clean machines
process the flesh coolly as hospitals.
Racks of knives and pans; fruit
and veg packed like wounds in gauze and ice.
Coffee beans in a glass jar: black
polished wooden beads that
slide through my hands, a broken rosary.
Our host invokes bones: risotto
with marrow, osso buco, boiled broth.
His wife hands ladles.

In the Faculty Club at nine
a silver lake of water in each glass, a
circular steel plaque, mirrors the
mouths of baby-faced men talking
business over breakfast: bacon
and weak white toast, eggs fried sunny side up.
Fresh soap and sausages. Fingers
of red blossom tap at the window pane.

The cafe is cut from onyx and formica, full
of purple neon striplights, indigo balloons.
Blue linen tablecloths, a metal counter
the waitresses re-spray
to polish off the marks of espresso cups.
Sunburned youths gobble sfogliatelle with ricotta
discuss real estate, singles computer dating parties
with silk-clad girl execs spooning in Sweet'n'Low.

I bite at a muffin stained with blueberries.
Fear of the future
breaks and enters me.

from
Psyche and the hurricane (1991)

Il barone rampante

On the eve of the New Year feast
an army of amazon cooks
tackles his kitchen.

The dead salmon winks
from its pastry bier.
He retreats
from the stripped prawns
the boiling cauldrons of oil
stalks out
with rucksack and alpenstock.

Up through the snowy woods
he plots his complex way
unmapped, unmarked.
The man of the mountains
puts together a white
jigsaw with black cracks.

Warnings drip from the rocks.
The mountain man
who hides in the tops
of trees and
licks snow off bushes
has a tongue of ice.

His boots yelp over snow.
The dark jaw of the cave
juts like his when he mutters:
'Tell her to give me *sa chose*.'

The grotto's his true
house: bed of beech
leaves, table and chair
carried here on his back
his bag of poems.

He curls between stone lips
starving. The mountain
gulps him in.
One day he will never come out.

for Paula, mourning

The Museo Civico garden
is a coffin of snow.
Fresh scent of bitter privet.
The fountain halts.

Grief buckles itself onto you
like a new winter coat.
Sono una ragazza distrutta
you tell me. Your skin
topples away. Life
cuts you up
like a raw potato.

You hold a second funeral
alone, filling the room
with candles and flowers
on New Year's Eve
drinking champagne
from the best crystal glass.

Paula, museum-keeper
you catalogue the smell of loss
in corridors, in letters. You
exhibit absence. You
list the many categories
of worldly joy.
Kneeling to dust the floor
the way your mother did
you acquire
her gestures.

Paula, curator of memories
keeper of your parents' house
I tell you
your mother
will rise inside you
strongly as the moon.

The road to Trento
(for Sarah giving birth)

White dashes. White dots.
Two white strokes:
a pine tree; a roof.

White pockmarks and scars
on beech trunks. White Vs
on what must be mountains.

Snow, sifted exactly, catches
all horizontals, out-
lines them. White
blocked onto white.

Waves and flurries
of frost
repeat, repeat.
Branches
fling up and out
like quivering wires.

We force ourselves
gently
through the cold pass

like your child
toboganning on
your slope
the world turning
itself inside out

the world
turning around
the world
bearing down.

We come down
into the valley
of castles and vineyards
and small white fields
combed with a black comb.

The fruit trees are ice.
I hear your great shout.

found poem

Red stripes on casualties of conflict.
All full-timers welcome.

All marriages
should be loaded from the bottom drawer
working upwards
marked with your local bitter
maiden name if any.
This marriage is fitted with
an anti-tilt device.
Caution: dry riser inside.
Danger. Men working overtime.
Safety helmets are provided
for your protection
and must be worn.
Men working overhead
on these premises: as a rule
men are more muscular than women.
Women naturally burn off
their maiden names.

Doctors encourage women: build
up a bit more muscle, or multiples thereof
as safety holds when marriages are empty.

Men don't have the same pressure.
Sorry ladies! Doctors encourage women
in their heavy duty.
Please allow twenty-eight days
for delivery.
Love is sterilized
and supplied pre-packed.

The management regrets unmarried
card-carrying members only
make matters worse.

Poltergeist

In Holland Park
the houses yawn in pastels.
Pink ironed girls, plaits under boaters
are swept to school in Volvos
by clean fathers popping to the City.
Speechless *au pairs* and babies
push off to the park. Mothers
gulp gin
at elevenses
in cool tiled kitchens of Italian décor.

Outside each house
a man in blue
cap and jacket sits
bent over, wide-
legged on the pavement.
The stone seams burst apart:
urgent delivery
Into his patient hands.
He clutches a bright snarl of colours:
fistfuls of spiralling current
jump in his lap, an electric bouquet.

Jollity sloshes along the patios
at dusk. Beasts roast on barbecues.
Fathers in sports shirts
spear cocktail onions. Mothers
give sloppy ice grins.

In the stitched-up street
the pavements bear traces
of fresh cement scars. The *au pairs*
blue as aerograms patrol
the nurseries. All thumbs
they spell today's vocabulary
the next explosion.

Restoration work in Palazzo Te

Psyche, imprisoned in the paint, has
got free, and wields a bucket. White
vest against her golden
shoulders, white overalls rolled
about her waist, she caresses
her sisters' eyes with a wet sponge.

Return to that house of desire
made flesh. Re-vision it. Discard
the cradle of winds, all magical escorts.
Prefer to be engineer
locking your steps to the air
on scaffolding frames
clasped with rusty latches.

She stares at the dream. Level after level
of images falls past. She clambers up
four ladders of narrative
till she swings free
in the vault of darkness, the
silence between sentences.

She's equipped with a photo-map
topped by a plastic sheet she
marks with a Pentel pen. Knocking
at the plaster of the myth's crust
she listens for disturbances
below the surface.

Now she is close to the invisible god:
pressing her ear to a deep crack
she hears him breathing.

Leaning over him, daring and disobedient
she hoists her lamp, clips it
to a metal strut, switches
the beam of her love full on.

At this point, the story breaks up:
the wall stutters, incoherent
in a litter of paint flakes.

She records that the presence of the male body
in the text disrupts it.
Here lies, she guesses, Eros:
her hero, naked and unconscious.

Her task is to rescue what she can
from the fresco: not
to smooth-talk; not to make him up.
Woken by her hot look, he sulks. He
never asked for this, resists

her questioning hands, her
fingers pattering at him, white
braille in white dust.

Possibly she's absurd.
Anyway, it is the work that matters.

The visit

A garden in full flood
brims at the windowsill.
Squares of transparent glass
press back green light, a
green sea, from white walls.

The red
kitchen submarine
carries a cargo of wine and
eggs, fresh cardamom.

Nosing past violent
hedges and grass, the
drip, drip of white
lilac, white roses
we lay out
our card-words.
Kali means *hot*. A
stranger, an angel
dances and burns
on the tip of my tongue.

I sleep in a high bed
pillowed on hills. Clouds
slide in, sidle
over the blue blanket.

In the night, piano music
rises up through the still house
and the silence, grows
like a swift tree
inventing
the tall well
of the spiralling stairs.

Then the cool notes
break and
fall, scatter
white petals in the darkness.

The return

This cathedral is God's
great whorled ear. Under
a roof of giant cockleshells
sung prayers stream
up, shoals of bright fish
flicking through water
over pebbles of stained glass.

This is my father's country
I've entered. This
is my father's house
– the Anglican one – I scorned:
its prim hats
and habits, its
grenadier parsons, its
teapot God.

I'm back, Dad! Your
prodigal daughter
in a shiny black mac
with my battered
heart, my suitcase of poems.

Sssh. There is a wedding
going on here
in a swarm of red
deaconesses
a roar of choirs.

My father leaps up
in the high space
and the mother I thought was lost
ricochets
round him. Strong
arches and vaults of flesh
enclose them. These
two make the sculpted air.
They are the architects. This
design is their dance.

I believe in the big ribbed boat
of the upturned church.
I believe in the body:
the house
the man and woman build
with the sweat of love.

A harvest journey

July was for undoing: I unpicked
my dark blue wedding dress
snipping at it stitch
by sorry stitch. What
to make of it?
Suddenly my hands
opened and my lap
emptied, letting
all those yards of heavy cotton go.

Wet September under Mendip
smelled of hot straw
and cow dung. Yellow
pears, bird-pecked, plummeted
to black earth sprouting
peppery nasturtiums.
The hills left the garden
in one blue fell swoop.

I helped my father pick and chop
apples and onions for chutney
prune the beech tree
with ladder and long shears.
He coughed rough spittle
into his handkerchief. My
mother complained the tall
branches were cruelly
lopped, that Dad's leeks
had wooden hearts. The string beans
quarrelled with the runners, the pot
clanged while the iron hissed.
I cooked omelettes, a sort of blessing.

Ploughs in Devon
stripped the great
valleys' flanks
back to the rich red bone.
Bullocks fattened for the butcher.
My days were bounded by thick strips
of coloured light, curves
of water, of shining rain

the smile and frown
of Dad in his old brown sweater
bringing bowls of spinach
and lettuces in.

Psyche and the hurricane

Freak weather
the forecasters called it, that
the computers couldn't catch.

In the dark single eye
of the storm
dedicated, intent

this island was found
offensive, to be
plucked out.

Some hasty goddess
tossed trees like cabers
tore strips off houses

set electricity loose.
So the white seas rose
to bang the prison-ship

against the rocks
till its belly split, spilt
out the bruised refugees.

I slept through it all in London
woke only to the tinkle
of breaking glass

though in my dreams
wanting letters, wanting
love, I heard her uproar.

From the train I saw the sky fall
onto the flooded
fields, pewter-blue

sun whiten the factory
windows, a hawthorn
burn red and yellow.

The grasses by the slagheaps
bloomed with light:
they were heavy with it.

In Leeds a red-headed woman
taught me a form
of patience, a pagan one:

how to cut coloured bits
from my chaotic
darkness, name and arrange them.

On Monday, in Essex
I counted the local damage:
the beech tree smashed onto the church

porch, the two Scotch firs
crushing the house opposite
the polluted sludge from the estuary

silting up windowsills
the roofs that simply vanished
leaving gaps of flat disbelief.

Wivenhoe Park was choked
by corpses, reclining.
The wind had wrung their necks

dangling and snapped, wrenched
ancient horse-chestnuts' roots
up out of great pits

laid them out, naked and dead
at loggerheads. Then the funerals
began, with fire, the whine of chainsaws.

I have lost Eros. My love
has been ripped
out, leaving me

shaped to this emptiness.
When I remember
his mouth on my breast

that startling current
jumps live again.
I'm un-earthed, I could be

dangerous. The red-headed woman
deals out my tasks. Number
one: face loneliness.

She sends me back to work
on the wind
with her blessing.

On midwinter night

You can't
summon an angel.

You can't
force the miraculous light
to slide from the star
and pierce your ear.

You have to give up
expecting it.

The proud girl
available to every
friend, belonging
to no one, she
has to sit
alone in the kitchen's
red stir of silence .
admitting her emptiness.

How can this be enough?
All she has to offer:
two open hands
no one might need.

She wants to promise
the one she can't see
she'll attempt to be ready.

A breath on her neck.
Her back, arched like a cat's
tries to jump away.

Why me? she bristles
to the blur of wings:
choose someone else!

Her assent
imprints her with
imagination's truth:

the angel re-enters her.

She watches the coffee-pot
start to shine, the edge
of the sugar bowl jiggle
with life. She carries
her future
carefully
inside herself: the words
she will share
with Elizabeth.

Going into Cornelissen's, Great Russell Street

The window held
jointed wooden
dolls: idols; the
toys of artists; it
drew me in.

The entrance: deep
as the tunnel
leading to that boy-king's
tomb; gilded
box within box, the
high doors
of his outermost skin
guarded by two still jackals
his entrails and heart packed
tight in
alabaster
canopic jars, the
square coffer tenderly braced
by four little
golden goddesses, one
at each corner, their
outstretched arms long as wings
their fingertips
touching each other's.

That moment
when the furthest cave
suddenly becomes a shrine
because the god is there.
I blinked on a blare of colour I
couldn't chew or swallow:
his invisible face
a dazzle of ground paint
incarnate, purely material.

Ranked on the shelves
fat bottles of clear
glass collected the light
separately, and
classified it, like
alphabets, or musical notes:
to render it bearable.

There were jars
transparent with the word *blue*:
turquoise, brilliant and sifted
violet, soft as chiffon
the iridescent pearl salts
of mauve and ultramarine.

Then an ampoule of orange henna
jazzed with saffron
yellow as wet sand
a staff of coffee, of *pain brûlé*
dissolved to contralto
rose, to
a screech of lime sorbet.

Flaring across the shop
the colours and light
burnt onto my retina
the dark of my eyelids
my heart.

Staggering
under the impact of the god
I found all the world
alive, refracted
inside me:
I composed
love's radiance
and held him.

A psalm for Easter

(for Jamila Embarek)

I

This was the night
when the chosen people
journeyed out of Egypt
towards the promised land.

This was the night
when the Red Sea parted
to give them safe passage
out of captivity.

This was the night
when the new fire
burned in the darkness
and the darkness could not extinguish it.

This was the night
when blood was smeared on the doorposts
when the Word burst from the sealed tomb
and out of death delivered us.

II

You gave to me.
You made me remember
my mother

how love
lugged her across the water
and made her strong

how she gave herself up
how she let life rip her
apart, in the name of love

how she gave birth
in a cold foreign town
alone, among strangers

how her son died on the third day
and was buried
and did not rise again.

III

You hung your arms
around our necks.

You slumped between us
your head on Pat's breast

and then on mine.
We held you up

on the edge of the metal bed.
We were your witnesses.

How you laboured
night into day into night

how dolorously
the delivery room

contracted to
pains that skewered you.

You thirsted. We laid
our wet fingers against your lips.

You clutched our hands
and didn't let go:

you cried out in Arabic and French
your mother-tongue, and mine

sometimes for your mother
and sometimes for me.

You doubted. You disbelieved.
You called for a knife

to cut you, quickly:
my husband, my husband

why have you abandoned me?
At the end, you abandoned yourself:

you put yourself to death.
You delivered yourself up:

then your son flashed out
like a fish, across the green sheet.

You turned your head away.
It was finished.

IV

This was the night
outside the hospital
when the milkman's cart
clattered in the frosty street.

This was the night
when four men in white walked past us
lighting the dark suburb
with four bright candle flames.

This was the night
the full moon hung above us
low and heavy as your breast
dented like your baby's head.

This was the night
I dreamed of a derelict old woman
her sodden nappy of newspapers
interleaved with poems.

This was the night
I learned the weight of sorrow
the weight of the sad body
my hands could hold.

V

They hung you, my daughter
on a metal cross.

From your precious wound
your blood fell out

thickly, collected in a bucket.
The green-gowned Sister

sat between your legs.
Where she had cut you

she stitched you up.
She wove you back together

with black threads. With her needle
she repaired the damage.

Then we unstrapped you
and took you down.

Then we laid you
unconscious, to rest.

VI

You gave to me.
You made me remember
my mother

and how I mourned, being born
alive, being born a daughter
how I thought I broke her, being born

how I wanted to break her again
and make her mourn
how I too was broken

how I was Egypt, that sad land
how I was the sealed tomb
with dead words inside.

You made me remember
how the mother must mourn the lost son
how the daughters must mourn

the lost mother, must ask
for forgiveness, how the daughters
must find and tend

the broken body of love
must mend it, must make
reparation.

VII

On the morning of the third day
love rose up early
inside the tomb.

Love breathed in my ear
and lifted me.
Love set me upright.

Then love rolled the stone away.
Then love opened my mouth.
Then love made me rise.

And I, who had died in this life
was born back into it.
I, who had died, was risen.

And she whom I had been searching for
was there. She was with me.
She was love's body:

alive
made whole again
in me.

In the New Year

A green tree in the dark house.
Hard buds of coloured light
stripped off it
at Epiphany, the
solid coffin
of the lopped spruce
carted out
by two of us, dumped
onto gravel.

Fourteen children
lay on the hill holding hands
in a ring
under a streak of stars
wishing for
one pulse, one
red dawn body.

The leaving train
tracked Devon's lip
licked and
bitten by sea.
As the sun jumped up
the silk of the mud flats
was amethyst
the world suddenly flushed
fat with radiance.

It all heaved up in me:
love, sobs, knowledge
the closeness of hedges and grass
how the one body was both of us.

In London
cold beads of water
marbled the indigo glass night.
The hyacinths
unclenched blue fists.
You delved in, rooting
me till
our dark body sparked with light.

The day the wall came down

1

We began as one
pram with two hoods
a secret language
a single dent in the bed.

At eleven plus
we failed at arithmetic
simple division
the test of love.

I thought you'd got all the heart
that I'd gobbled your brain.

To keep myself in
I had to keep you out:
our free air
hardened to glass
unscratchable.

The times were un–nourishing.
There was one too many:
it was you or me.

You thinned yourself
down to bone
broth. Your hair fell out.
Your toes and fingers turned blue.
I was white fat, pork belly
I was mash and grease.

Both of us
made ourselves scarce.
Our conjuring trick:
our disappearing needs.

Sometimes, from far away
I'd holler
into your silence, at
our sad milk.

2

Our date: astonishing November
near Euston
an oven-basement
where lunch
eats up the afternoon

and we chew over
the babies you've got
the baby I dreamed I'd steal

and you feed me advice fresh
and gritty as pepper, necessary
as salt

my sister in black and silver
your breath close, your
face flushed with wine

and we taste garlic, spaghetti
anchovies, broccoli
hot with red chillies

and what has divided us
comes down

the work of our mouths
desirous
eating, meeting.

3

Twins with our guards
torn down: now
we reclaim
each other's hidden city
as our own, the
other side of skin.

Foreign as freedom
on my new route back

to slip on the silvery
grease of pavements
smell the secret life of Camden
feel the electric blue
bruise of the evening sky
over the railway lines
of Kentish Town

where cafés offer honeycakes
the tick of dominoes
contact with strangers'
eyes idling by TV screens

and greengrocers' caves
are dark mouths, bearded
with cloths of grass
moustached by swags of brilliant
bulbs, pearl onions.

In my arms rustle papery
sheaths: inky irises
unfurl their blue fur tongues
anemones in mud–coloured ruffs
open their fat black eyes
a shout of purple.

All the way home
I listen to
the morse code of
woodpeckers

my sister calling for
me through the cold
years, the

tapping
of the axes
of love.

4

The pour of bodies.
The gap.

Memorial
to that which is still missing
all that which longs to be said.

Lacrimae rerum

Another leak
in the lavatory roof
drip drip down the lightbulb.
I pissed in the dark, raindrops
smacking my shoulder-blades.

This morning I woke
to fresh wet birdsong
under a cloud of quilt
last night's hot sweetness
still fizzing between my legs.

I was fooled into swallowing spring
jumping up to make tea
and rinse dishes, whistle
a liquid kitchen oratorio.

It's your birthday next week.
This time next year
I think you'll be gone
quietly as this water
slipping over my hands.

After your funeral
we'll return
to your parched house.
We'll try to hold our mother up
like this exhausted roof.

I carry your dying
inside me
as real as milk

as I'll carry on
getting the roof fixed
making love
weeping into the washing-up.

A walk on the south downs

In January
even the wind is lean
trimming the hawthorns
to blunt, bent doggedness

scraping the downs
out; hollow
vistas of hunger
a morphine fast.

Your body is
a die that
stamps
these hills: the stretch
of your pain
repeatedly
struck into soft chalk.

Jim and I
flounder up
valleys of mud
bulky as elephants
clotting our boots

winter slapping loose
lips together: mud
swallows, mud belch.

So easy, in this tired air
to let go your hand
the hedgerows' whippy support
yield, slide
to that sucking bed

not to plod on, haul
our legs
to the top
of the tunnelling path

tip ourselves out
over the gate
onto sheep-nibbled
tumbledown slopes

where the long man
rests, the
sunset under his feet
his outline restored in white chalk
his empty belly full of fresh grass.

mayday mayday

The fields here tick over
with dandelion clocks
fragile and full
as luminous as moons.

Your room smells of fish and shit.
You curl in your nightie
a clack of bones.
Your guts are plastic
gartered to your thin thigh.

Down the lane the maypole
shakes out its ribbons
on pointed toes.
Solemn and quick
the children's knees skip up.
Sandals and anoraks.
Print frocks as
sharp as lettuces. Your
death dances forwards. Your
death dances back.

I do what I can:
bleed the fridge dry
hack up the chicken for soup
rip milky weeds from the grass.

You thrash on.
Death's hooks in
your belly, your mouth.

You're so pale. Parched
as these London streets
cracking up in the heat.

The butcher's in Holloway Road
gusts forth the smell of warm blood.

Your voice on the telephone
stumbles: so far away.

I slept in your attic
looking over the long hill.
The open window let in
cold sweet darkness
impersonal stars
sheep crying in the night.

marking time

Midsummer's Day.
The darkest.
Red growls of poppies.
Skies in the afternoon
blacken like spoiled wheat.

A clutch of women
in the kitchen mixes
tears and
shoulders, the remains
of a hot roast dinner.

You're a skull on the pillows
two hands that
jerk and grope
in receding air
to the pulse of the drug-
pump, a
mutter: *it's so strange.*

I kiss your soft blistered lips.
Leaving.
Trying to let go.
I blurt out: *you won't
kick the bucket just yet.*
You smile at me:
oh yes I think I will.

Our mother stays with you.
Must watch

day by day
your life torn off
you, red
poppy petals.

for Jackie

We're back
in the old
house, the one on cine-film:
Dad in his shirt-sleeves
grinning, Mum
with her hair pinned up
her short fur jacket.

You haven't left.
And now
there's a verandah
at the front:
half-in, half-out
your bed of glass.

You sit up, lively.
Arms outstretched.
In conversation.
What joy, sister
to see you lucid.

Uncles and aunts and cousins
fill up the room behind.
A sort of party.
I'm expecting twins.

I wake in my own
bed. Thirsty.
I haven't slept.
Dreaming about you all night.

Cold water in a cup.
The kitchen glimmers. Gold
sucks me up
feet on a chair, headfirst
through the attic skylight.
Dawn breaks like red glass.

The phonecall comes at seven.

You died in your sleep
as the day began.

morning delivery

He arrives too early
the back of his lorry
stacked with black booty.

A mask and gloves of soot.
Ten menacing sacks
lounge on the path.
He says he's been ordered
to shoulder these bully-boys in.

Already
he's taken the lid off
the coal cellar's mouth
by the front steps.

I stumble underground.
Start shovelling.

Daylight's round eye
level with mine
is blacked
out. Coal's relentless fists
pummel the earth floor.
Knobbles of darkness
roar past my knees
in a rubble tide.

Forced food of
dust. The cellar chokes.

A loose black hill
collapses in my house.
Black landslide

cold as the torrent
bearing you along

my sister
in a long box

to be burnt up
swallowed into black ash.

new poems (1992–1995)

At Alfriston

The lilac pushes
white at us:
white smoke of
incense cones, the
curly bulk, bitten into
of pearls and rice.

White scatters itself:
crinkle of cowparsley
in ditches
moonbeads of daisies, milk-
drops in the long grass.

Raised knots of white braid
fasten the darkness
of chestnut trees.
White posies jiggle and tilt.

The hawthorns
are dredged in white. Flare
of white fireworks
in the black
hedge–
cracks between fields.

The path is a white parting
a chalk line going up
deep cut in the green wheat.

The downs round whiteness out.
Here's the fall
of a cowslip hill
into our hands

the white trace of a god.

the wedding party

it was a May journey
to the downs' fullness
their hot brown distances

ripple of
white paths: flung
bolts of
bleached
calico

larks kept the sky up
billowy blue tent
with beaks, whirring wings
a pole of song

under our feet
a helter-skelter
rattle: marine-veined flints
dividing the green wheat

then the fall
to a steep chalk valley
of yellow gorse
fierce as blisters
lapped by cowslip quilts

a gold satin pennant
pointed at the noon sun

the wedding party
came walking over the hill
a rabble of saints

in Indian muslin skirts
cord waistcoats
and top hats

they carted plaited wicker baskets
cloths, cakes, the green necks of wine

the straw-hatted bridegroom
was nearly eighty
his eyes merry and serene

his bride, now seventy
wore a crown of anemones on her white hair

re-discovering Pompeii

(an exhibition at the Accademia Italiana, London)

i

you only had half your life
death jumped in and snatched you away

still in dreams
I give birth to you
so long waited for

night into day
months into years
turning

my hidden daughter
my daughter who disappeared

you are buried in me
I am very patient, I endure
I hold you, emptiness
you dent me, I am your mould

ii

mountain you broke loose again
mountain you tipped yourself out

no stopping you
the red slide of your insides

these walled streets became
your arteries
your throat
your burning tongue

thick river of red lava
flowed from you, volcano

houses were beakers
brimmed with red fire

you stoppered
their open mouths
with seething mud

your hands of wind
scattered red fragments
you let fly

you spent yourself
you cooled and hardened
the city was silent

soon the dead were forgotten
soon you forgot

iii

who is she
this woman of resin
darkly transparent
twisted and glistening

body flung facedown
she tripped while fleeing
a finger of gas pushed her over
she choked on hot ash

then lava covered her

she vanished
she was the space inside
she was the secret:

loss is solid

iv

in the corners
of the exhibition hall
the computers hold court

screens talk back
to our fingertip touch
calmly they instruct us
I cannot stroke your face

v

the catalogue
cannot utter this:

inside me
in my heart's house
in the scorching flow
of lava and tears

you are preserved
for evermore

my daughter of injected resin
my daughter of glued terracotta
my daughter of pierced silver
of apple-green glass

my tongue is broken
you mend me
you rise up
you restore yourself to me
out of the pit of winter

The Aunt's Progress

I

house of night whispers
between sisters
house of wasted flesh

scarred house
cut and stitched house
house of your rasping breath

hide-and-seek house
hunt-the-aunt house
cat-and-mouse house

house of the uninvited guest

II

behind your bedroom door
a roar of cold air
buffets my ears
slaps me back

who's this impostor
laid out on your bed
sheet stretched taut
from chin to toe

this sly arrival
nose in the air
so secretive
all closed up
impossibly still

who let her in
this chalk-faced mime
her eyelids as smug as eggs
implacable, dumb
under a shutter of skin

any minute now
she'll unstifle her laugh
and look
she'll speak
this fake, this replica

this scarecrow with sparse hair
who feigns sleep
this effigy, this doll

III

at 2 a.m.
your absence knocks in the roof
gurgles along the pipes
from room to room

tap tap tap
are you there

below my stiff pillow
the hum of that chill machine
the jumpy tread of the stairs

tap tap tap
are you there

IV

on the fourth day
the men in black
arrive to wheel her out
in her wooden pram

they get her as far as the hall
this impersonator of aunts
in her rotten disguise
her mask of greenish wax

she's on display
tucked up in brown nylon
quilts, incorrupt
an imitation saint
her porcelain head sunk deep
her bonnet
of white padding
narrow as a nun's

the men collect her, their prize
wadded in cotton
boxed up, presentable

whoever she is
they slide on the lid
they pull her away

V

from the house
we deliver you, *marraine*

into these men's hands
the hands of the undertakers
the grave-diggers
the priests

out of this life
we deliver you

to be churched
praised, blessed, borne off
prayed for, and buried

so that fear may finish
and grief may begin

VI

your parents were your windows
your shutters, your walls
you built yourself to their plan
on their foundation

when they removed
to death
the house shook, shivered
bits and pieces
of yourself fell off
never to be recovered

first your breast left you
then your hair
it was practical
the collapsing flesh
your life leaked out of you
into bedpans
white enamel kidney dishes

VII

in Le Havre
in the pink-floored hospital
you gagged on plastic
you couldn't speak

your great eyes
testified
made your statement
to us, your witnesses

you tried to collect yourself
your long finger wagged *no*
at the misplaced gauze
the crease in the clean towel

but the chairs jumped about
gulls from the docks
zigzagged their cries
above your bed
needy people
clopped in and out
they bristled with gifts
gladioli whose colours hurt
crème caramel you couldn't eat

we tipped into you
one drop of water at a time
between your lips
from the tilted spoon

your sister became your mother
she held on to you
throughout the night
of that lost summer

you whispered:
it's difficult to die

VIII

I skulk back
to your unhomely house
which holds my breath
these disturbances of air

the ghost moves in
close, only a skin away

she tickles my spine
through invisible swing doors
she squats my grandmother's chair
keeps watch
over peeling paint
empty picture hooks

that haunted child
for forty years
I hushed her
her unnameable wish

she waits for darkness
she leans over my bed
slides in
too frightened for crying
refugee from punishment

that cold white woman downstairs
resurrects herself
an avenger in marble
rises
jumps up the steep stairs
hovers just beyond the keyhole

crash
the mirror breaks
down, into the basin
shards tumble like water
daggers of ice
all the selves I was

IX

for our last outing
to Etretat
Margi and I hauled you
between us, frogmarched
your legs of wool
you were gleeful:
those smart people
will think I'm drunk

onto the beloved beach
propped you on the stone hill
bandaged with scarves and coats
lay back, all three
salt on our lips, into seaweed smells
sun stroked the water
the cliffs threw themselves
out, deep in, down

never before had we sat together so long
never before had we sat together so still

in silence
the blue-green sea
drawing us forward
pushing us back

till the shops had all shut
the fish for supper was not got
you sang out never mind
you wanted to stay

your life
still goes
on sliding
in and out
of mine

back and forth
the sea on these stones
rubbing itself out

repeatedly

writing itself in on me
over and over

X

here, on this empty edge
the sky falls down
around me

the crumpled bulk
of the cliffs

collapsed cathedrals

granite parachutes
billow to folds and
settle, are still

you're free now
of thrift and chemotherapy and dust

you're gone and can never return

you're one with these
splinters of water
this gull-filled air

XI

wild violets and anemones
glow like planets
in the night-green woods

a deer rises
from rosy bracken
races across the track

through the rain
a slippery sun
gleams oyster-wet

a solid bend of colours
leaps over the house

which smells of breakfast
of chocolate and bread
of salt and yeast

maternal

out of the back door
the bulk of washed linen
is heaved in baskets

wet weight of cotton
in unmanageable lengths
bunched up in my arms

tumbles down free
a soft wall
pinched between fingertips

stretched out taut
jerked away
swung up

smacked and shaken
by the hands
of the wind

truant laundry
that struggles and kicks

cartwheeling washing
which pouts and dances

small white acrobats
juggle pegs
hang on by their teeth
to the whipcrack line

tethered to it
tugging
loose, gripping tight

sun–dried, fresh–smelling
lively and wild as children

as those lucky ones
who can be found
fetched, gathered up
pressed to the heart

carried safely in

birthday in Istanbul

in the beginning
a buzz of golden darkness
hollowed from air

quartz crystals
in the split rock

the sculptor bees
cluster and hum
in their basilica hive

praising
its honeycomb galleries
of marble vaults

its drip of mosaics
gold-encrusted

these tender arches
of lapis–lazuli
burning blue

and now this
somersault in stone

double back–flip up
to the enclosing dome

the god with her godchild
floats
on a jewelled trapeze

rolling the sun
on her shoulders
in a gold sack

she beats her resonant skin drum
it rises, that song inside

give birth to me
I want to be born

house-hunting in the Mayenne

all the windows
of these village
houses
flop our their red tongues
of geraniums

inside the Lion d'Or
on orange chenille
I mouth new wants and
lap at you
milk–white
sour–sweet

you're my house
as I am yours
founded on rock
the hillside at our back

diving inside
soft walls of flesh

we open up
rooms of secret words
pungent   scarlet   hot

going to the Marché de la Poésie in Paris

sun striped the sweltering alleys
criss-crossing the hedged box
of the Jardin de Luxembourg

choirs of black treetrunks
parched
gasped out staccato chants
of heat cool heat

the honey scent of lime
blossom drenched us
under clipped awnings
of massed green leaves

manna-drops, a
rainfall of flowers
pale as acacia or camomile
crinkled tissue-paper twists

fisted like a first draft
scrunched-up as these women's
tea-coloured muslin dresses
puckered back over
curves of bare knees
parted and

poised on iron chairs
that posed like sphinxes
pawed the packed sand
brown as coffee with milk

while in the Place St Sulpice
tides of books and poets
pushed through an island-maze
of emerald kiosks
neat as beach-huts

with open doors and silver
corrugated-metal
roofs: ovens to cook up poems

ink sweated off paper
onto caressing hands
the edges of pages dissolved
to smells of
vanilla and oranges like a lover's skin

the Angelus bells
unloosed their tongues and
drowned the metro's roar
fathoms deep under pavement grilles

the electric lavender sky
fell up and down around
the tiny plane
thunder-dandled

red wine lifted out of glasses
fountain plumes
that splashed benediction
onto neighbouring laps

lightning scrawled neon words
all over us
we translated at home to
cries of bliss crackling in the dark

Other books of interest

WE, THE DANGEROUS

Janice Mirikitani

'A major poet in America, Janice Mirikitani speaks all our truths' — *Maya Angelou*

Janice Mirikitani writes with a powerful and uncompromising poetic vision about a range of subjects — from the internment experience, which silenced her own family and many second generation Japanese Americans, to the Gulf War. Dramatic, lyrical and always intense, her work takes poetry into new and dangerous realms:

She could do anything with a knife./ Gut shrimp/ with a single slice/ dice/ an onion before a tear/ could slide/ . . . Some say she was cut deep/ when her GI split/ and left her/ in the middle of America./ She couldn't go back home/ in disgrace/ so she carved out a place,/ her one counter cafe/ long before sushi/ became fashionable to jade junkies/ . . . Yea, they'd stand in line/ to see her magic/ with a knife/ scale,/ skin/ slice/ dice/ chop/ And they'd always ask,/ Do you orientals do everything so neatly?

Janice Mirikitani is published in Britain for the first time in this selection of poems old and new.

ROTTEN POMERACK

Merle Collins

At the heart of this fiercely haunting volume of poems is an ardent spirit of storytelling. Voices whisper or shout or quietly call attention to some particular experience, whether personal or political — the longing for 'home' wherever it may be and the balm of forgetting. For the women and men in these poems, their stories begin in the Caribbean and move to England (*'nearly ten years later/look me here analysing/still distraught and debating/sympathising synthesising/regretting and remembering/and time just passing'*). These poems are about the ironies and paradoxes of living — the proverbial slipping on a 'rotten pomerack' (French-Creole for the cashew fruit) which can make events take an unexpected turn — but most of all they are poems that break the listening silence.

HARAKU / LOVE POETRY
New and Selected Love Poems

June Jordan

'Jordan makes us think of Akhmatova, of Neruda. She is among the bravest of us, the most outraged. She feels for all. She is the universal poet.' – *Alice Walker*

The pain, the vulnerability and the erotic sweetness of love glow brilliantly at the heart of this volume of poetry. The Haraku poems dip and dove-tail taking from the haiku its purity and economy, but giving them a vision that is June Jordan's own. Every poem is a bud or bursting flower imbued with the most complex images as well as an aching desire to put right the whole Asian-American experience. The other poems are selected from volumes published over the last twenty years. Together they bring to love poetry a new and more urgent definition.

THE COMPLETE COLLECTED POEMS OF MAYA ANGELOU

Maya Angelou

'You will hear the regal women; the mischievous street girl
... Black, bitter and beautiful, she speaks of our survival'
—*James Baldwin*

'Maya Angelou writes from the heart and her language
rings clear and true . . . whether joyful or playful, her poems
speak with delicacy and depth of feeling' – *M.F.K. Fisher*

Published for the first time in one exuberant volume, Maya
Angelou's poetry is just as much a part of her life as her famous
autobiography. With lyrical and dramatic skill, she winds skeins of
longing and desire, throws punches – tough and tender – as she
writes about freedom and shattered dreams. Her profound and
inspiring poem, 'On the Pulse of Morning', written for President
Clinton's inauguration, is also included. History in the making,
heartbreak and freedom – these are Maya Angelou's themes so
richly explored in cadences and rhythms of infinite inventiveness.

Forthcoming poetry from Virago

MORNING IN THE BURNED HOUSE

Margaret Atwood

'A novelist and poet of great gifts' – *Guardian*

'Margaret Atwood . . . deserves an adjective – Atwoodian – in recognition of her virtuoso wit and unmistakable style' – *Chicago Tribune*

By turns dark, playful, intensely moving, tender and intimate – these poems are Atwood's most accomplished, mature and versatile, 'setting foot on the middle ground / between body and word'. Here is that wickedly dry, humorous voice – Helen of Troy appears as a tabletop dancer, Miss July muses on life as a cheesecake queen and Cressida reveals what she really thought of Troilus. And here too are personal poems that concern themselves with love, with memory, with the fragility of the natural world. A beautiful elegiac series of meditations on the death of a parent, completes this generous and disturbing collection of wonderful, rare poems.